2010 SOC User Guide

U.S. Bureau of Labor Statistics
On behalf of the Standard Occupational Classification Policy Committee (SOCPC)

February 2010

2010 SOC User Guide

U.S. Bureau of Labor Statistics
On behalf of the Standard Occupational Classification Policy Committee (SOCPC)

February 2010
Questions should be emailed to soc@bls.gov

Contents

Introduction   ii

What's New in the 2010 SOC   vi

Classification Principles   xii

Coding Guidelines   xiii

Standard Occupational Classification and Coding Structure   xiv

Approved Modifications to the Structure   xviii

Frequently Asked Questions   xx

Acknowledgements   xxvii

Introduction

Purpose of the Standard Occupational Classification

The 2010 Standard Occupational Classification (SOC) system is used by Federal statistical agencies to classify workers and jobs into occupational categories for the purpose of collecting, calculating, analyzing, or disseminating data.

Users of occupational data include government program managers, industrial and labor relations practitioners, students considering career training, job seekers, career and employment counselors, educational institutions, and employers wishing to set salary scales or to locate to a new facility. Federal agencies use the SOC system to collect occupational data. The implementation of the 2000 SOC meant that for the first time, all major occupational data sources produced by the Federal statistical system provided data that are comparable, greatly improving the usefulness of the data. The 2010 SOC continues to serve this purpose and has been revised to improve data collection and maintain currency.

The SOC is designed to reflect the current occupational structure of the United States; it classifies all occupations in which work is performed for pay or profit. The SOC covers all jobs in the national economy, including occupations in the public, private, and military sectors. All Federal agencies that publish occupational data for statistical purposes are required to use the SOC to increase data comparability across Federal programs. State and local government agencies are strongly encouraged to use this national system to promote a common language for categorizing and analyzing occupations.

To facilitate classification and presentation of data, the SOC is organized in a tiered system with four levels, ranging from major groups to detailed occupations. There are 23 major groups, broken into 97 minor groups. Each minor group is broken into broad groups, of which there are 461. There are, at the most specified level, 840 detailed occupations. Detailed occupations in the SOC with similar job duties, and in some cases skills, education, and/or training, are grouped together. Each worker is classified into only one of the 840 detailed occupations based on the tasks he or she performs.

Overview of SOC Manual 2010

The *SOC Manual 2010* manual describes the occupational structure showing the different levels of aggregation, as well as the occupation titles and definitions. Illustrative examples of job titles used in an occupation are listed. The *SOC Manual 2010* also discusses the principles of classification, guidelines for coding jobs to the classification, and answers to Frequently Asked Questions. Detailed occupation descriptions and other information in the manual also can be found on the SOC homepage at http://www.bls.gov/soc. To obtain a CD-ROM version or additional print copies of the *SOC Manual 2010*, contact:

US Department of Commerce
National Technical Information Service
5301 Shawnee Road
Alexandria, VA 22312
(703) 605-6000 or 1-800-553-NTIS (6847)
Order Number: PB2010-105544 (hard cover)
Order Number: PB2010-500061 (CD-ROM)

Historical background

The Standard Occupational Classification (SOC) was first published in 1980, but was rarely used. The Office of Management and Budget (OMB) created the SOC Revision Policy Committee (SOCRPC) to revise the SOC for 2000 with the purpose of creating a system of classification that would allow all government agencies and private industry to produce comparable data.

Completed in 1998, the 2000 SOC resulted from 4 years of research by the SOCRPC and workgroups composed of members of more than 15 government agencies. The SOCRPC used the Bureau of Labor Statistics' (BLS) Occupational Employment Statistics (OES) occupational classification system as the starting point for the new SOC framework.

The *SOC Manual 2010* replaces the 2000 edition, and will be adopted by all Federal agencies that use the *SOC Manual 2000*.

Revision process for the 2010 edition

In 2005, the Office of Management and Budget first met with the Standard Occupational Classification Policy Committee (SOCPC) which includes representatives from the following agencies:

- o Department of Labor, Bureau of Labor Statistics and Employment and Training Administration
- o Department of Commerce, Census Bureau
- o Department of Defense, Defense Manpower Data Center
- o Department of Education, National Center for Education Statistics
- o Equal Employment Opportunity Commission
- o Department of Health and Human Services, Health Resources and Services Administration
- o National Science Foundation, Division of Science Resources Statistics
- o Office of Personnel Management
- o Office of Management and Budget, Office of Information and Regulatory Affairs

To initiate the formal 2010 SOC revision process, OMB and the SOCPC requested public comment in a May 16, 2006, *Federal Register* notice (71 FR 28536) on: (1) the Standard

Occupational Classification Principles, (2) corrections to the *Standard Occupational Classification Manual 2000*, (3) the intention to retain the current SOC major group structure, (4) changes to the existing detailed occupations, and (5) new detailed occupations to be added to the revised 2010 SOC.

To carry out the bulk of the revision effort, the SOCPC created six workgroups comprised of agency staff to examine occupations in the following major groups:

- o Management, Professional, and Related Occupations (major groups 11-29)
- o Service Occupations (major groups 31-39)
- o Sales and Office Occupations (major groups 41-43)
- o Natural Resources, Construction, and Maintenance Occupations (major groups 45-49)
- o Production, Transportation, and Material Moving Occupations (major groups 51-53) and
- o Military Specific Occupations (major group 55).

The workgroups were charged with reviewing comments received in response to the May 16, 2006, *Federal Register* notice (71 FR 28536) and providing recommendations to the SOCPC. Guided by the Classification Principles, the SOCPC reviewed the recommendations from the workgroups and reached decisions by consensus.

OMB announced the proposed new structure in a *Federal Register* notice on May 22, 2008 (73 FR 29930). OMB, in conjunction with the SOCPC, reviewed and carefully considered the comments received in response to these notices in the process of making its final decisions. The final 2010 occupation changes were announced in a *Federal Register* notice on January 21, 2009 (74 FR 3920).

Future of the SOC

The SOC Policy Committee will continue to serve as a standing committee after publication of the *SOC Manual 2010*, to perform maintenance functions such as recommending clarifications of SOC definitions, placement of new occupations within the existing structure, and updates to title files, including the newly-created Direct Match Title File.

The Direct Match Title File lists associated job titles for many detailed SOC occupations. Each of these titles is a direct match to a single SOC occupation. All workers with a job title listed in the Direct Match Title File are classified in only one detailed SOC occupation code. All Federal agencies that use the SOC will adopt the Direct Match Title File, although some may maintain separate program-specific title files. The Direct Match Title File, available on the SOC Web site at http://www.bls.gov/soc, allows data users to compare occupational information for these titles across Federal statistical agencies.

The SOCPC will continue to update the Direct Match Title File on a regular basis. Interested parties may suggest additional job titles to the SOCPC by e-mailing SOC@bls.gov.

The SOCPC has proposed that the next revision of the SOC will result in a 2018 edition, with the next major review and revision of the SOC expected to begin in 2013. The intent of this revision schedule is to minimize disruption to data providers, producers, and users by promoting simultaneous adoption of revised occupational and industry classification systems for those data series that use both. Given the multiple interdependent programs that rely on the SOC, this is best accomplished by timing revisions of the SOC for the years following North American Industry Classification System (NAICS) revisions, which occur for years ending in 2 and 7. The next such year is 2018, which has the additional benefit of coinciding with the beginning year of the American Community Survey 5-year set of surveys that bracket the 2020 Decennial Census. Thus, OMB intends to consider revisions of the SOC for 2018 and every 10 years thereafter.

What's New in the 2010 SOC

The 2010 SOC system contains 840 detailed occupations, aggregated into 461 broad occupations. In turn, the SOC combines these 461 broad occupations into 97 minor groups and 23 major groups. Of the 840 detailed occupations in the 2010 SOC, 359 remained exactly the same as in 2000, 453 had definition changes, 21 had a title change only, and 7 had a code change without a change in definition. Most of the definition changes (392) were editorial revisions that did not change occupational content. Therefore, no substantive changes occurred in occupational coverage for about 90 percent of the detailed occupations in the 2010 SOC.

Occupational areas with significant revisions and additions included

- Information technology (minor group 15-1100 Computer Occupations)
- Healthcare (major groups 29-0000 Healthcare Practitioners and Technical Occupations and 31-0000 Healthcare Support Occupations)
- Printing (minor group 51-5100 Printing Workers) and
- Human resources (minor group 13-1000 Business Operations Specialists)

In comparison to the 2000 SOC, the 2010 SOC realized a net gain of 19 detailed occupations, 12 broad occupations, and 1 minor group. The nature of the changes in detailed occupations is indicated in table 1.

Table 1: Distribution of detailed 2010 occupations, by type of change, 2000-2010

Type of change			2010 SOC detailed occupations	
Code changed?	Title revised?	Definition revised?	Number	Percent[1]
No	No	No	359	42.7
No	No	Yes[2]	356	42.4
No	Yes	Yes[2]	44	5.2
Yes	Yes	Yes[2]	42	5.0
No	Yes	No	21	2.5
Yes	No	Yes[2]	11	1.3
Yes	No	No	7	0.8
Yes	Yes	No	0	0.0
All occupations			840	100.0

[1] May not add to total due to rounding
[2] Of the 453 definition changes, 392 were editorial or to account for changes in technology. The remaining 61 occupations with revisions to definitions affected occupational coverage and are embedded in these rows. See page ix, Revised Occupational Definitions.

New occupations

The 2010 SOC contains 24 new occupations and codes that were broken out of the 2000 SOC occupations. These occupations are as follows:

2010 SOC

Code	*2010 SOC Title*
13-1131	Fundraisers
15-1122	Information Security Analysts
15-1134	Web Developers
15-1143	Computer Network Architects
15-1152	Computer Network Support Specialists
21-1094	Community Health Workers
25-2051	Special Education Teachers, Preschool
25-2059	Special Education Teachers, All Other
29-1128	Exercise Physiologists
29-1151	Nurse Anesthetists
29-1161	Nurse Midwives
29-1171	Nurse Practitioners
29-2035	Magnetic Resonance Imaging Technologists
29-2057	Ophthalmic Medical Technicians
29-2092	Hearing Aid Specialists
29-9092	Genetic Counselors
31-1015	Orderlies
31-9097	Phlebotomists
33-9093	Transportation Security Screeners
39-4031	Morticians, Undertakers, and Funeral Directors
43-3099	Financial Clerks, All Other
47-2231	Solar Photovoltaic Installers
49-9081	Wind Turbine Service Technicians
51-3099	Food Processing Workers, All Other

The number of detailed occupations (821) in the 2000 SOC increased to 845 with the addition of these 24 new occupations. The final count of 2010 SOC occupations (840) was due to a number of other changes.

- o The 2010 detailed occupation 51-9151 Photographic Process Workers and Processing Machine Operators resulted from combining two detailed 2000 occupations into one.
- o The 2010 detailed occupation 11-9013 Farmers, Ranchers, and Other Agricultural Managers resulted from combining two detailed 2000 occupations into one.
- o The 2010 detailed occupations in minor group 51-5110 Printing Workers, 51-5111 Prepress Technicians and Workers, 51-5112 Printing Press Operators, and 51-5113 Print Binding and Finishing Workers, resulted from combining five detailed 2000 occupations into three.
- o Three 2000 SOC computer occupations were revised to six detailed occupations in the 2010 SOC, four of which are included in the list of new occupations above.

For more information on the relationships between detailed occupations in the 2000 and 2010 SOC, see the crosswalks available in electronic format at http://www.bls.gov/soc.

Occupations that moved within the SOC structure

As another indicator of the scope of changes, the nine detailed occupations listed below moved from one major group in the 2000 SOC to another in the 2010 SOC.

- o Emergency Management Directors (11-9161) moved into major group 11-0000 Management Occupations from major group 13-0000 Business and Financial Operations Occupations, where it was previously Emergency Management Specialists (13-1061)

- o Farm Labor Contractors (13-1074) moved into major group 13-0000 Business and Financial Operations Occupations from major group 45-0000 Farming, Fishing, and Forestry Occupations

- o Fundraisers (13-1131) moved into major group 13-0000 Business and Financial Operations Occupations from Sales and Related Workers, All Other (41-9099) in major group 41-0000 Sales and Related Occupations

- o Market Research Analysts and Marketing Specialists (13-1161) moved into major group 13-0000 Business and Financial Operations Occupations from multiple SOC occupations including Market Research Analysts in major group 19-0000 Life, Physical, and Social Science Occupations and Public Relations Specialists in major group 27-0000 Arts, Design, Entertainment, Sports, and Media Occupations

- o Workers in the newly-created Transportation Security Screeners (33-9093) were previously classified in multiple SOC occupations including Compliance Officers, Except Agriculture, Construction, Health and Safety, and Transportation in major group 13-0000 Business and Financial Operations

- o Workers in the newly-created Morticians, Undertakers, and Funeral Directors (39-4031) were previously classified with Funeral Directors (11-9061) in major group 11-0000 Management Occupations

- o Workers in the newly-created Solar Photovoltaic Installers (47-2231) were previously classified in multiple SOC occupations including two in major group 49-0000 Installation, Maintenance, and Repair Occupations—Heating, Air Conditioning, and Refrigeration Mechanics and Installers (49-9021) and Installation, Maintenance, and Repair Workers, All Other (49-9099)

- o Flight Attendants (53-2031) moved into major group 53-0000 Transportation and Material Moving Occupations from major group 39-0000 Personal Care and Service Occupations

- o Transportation Attendants, Except Flight Attendants (53-6061) moved into major group 53-0000 Transportation and Material Moving Occupations from major group 39-0000 Personal Care and Service Occupations

Revised occupational definitions

There were 61 instances of revisions to definitions that affected occupational coverage. These 61 detailed occupations are listed below and include the 24 new occupations denoted by an asterisk (*). This list encompasses collapsed occupations, as well as 2010 occupations that resulted from a split. Other occupations had editorial changes or modifications to account for changes in technology. A table describing the nature of the changes, by detailed occupation, is available at http://www.bls.gov/soc.

2010 SOC Code	2010 SOC Title
11-9013	Farmers, Ranchers, and Other Agricultural Managers
11-9061	Funeral Service Managers
13-1041	Compliance Officers
13-1071	Human Resources Specialists
13-1075	Labor Relations Specialists
13-1121	Meeting, Convention, and Event Planners
13-1131	Fundraisers *
13-1161	Market Research Analysts and Marketing Specialists
13-1199	Business Operations Specialists, All Other
15-1121	Computer Systems Analysts
15-1122	Information Security Analysts *
15-1134	Web Developers*
15-1142	Network and Computer Systems Administrators
15-1143	Computer Network Architects *
15-1152	Computer Network Support Specialists *
21-1091	Health Educators
21-1094	Community Health Workers *
21-1099	Community and Social Service Specialists, All Other
23-1012	Judicial Law Clerks
23-2011	Paralegals and Legal Assistants
25-2051	Special Education Teachers, Preschool *
25-2052	Special Education Teachers, Kindergarten and Elementary School
25-2059	Special Education Teachers, All Other *
25-3099	Teachers and Instructors, All Other
27-3031	Public Relations Specialists
29-1128	Exercise Physiologists *
29-1129	Therapists, All Other
29-1141	Registered Nurses
29-1151	Nurse Anesthetists*
29-1161	Nurse Midwives *
29-1171	Nurse Practitioners *
29-2034	Radiologic Technologists
29-2035	Magnetic Resonance Imaging Technologists *
29-2057	Ophthalmic Medical Technicians *
29-2092	Hearing Aid Specialists *
29-2099	Health Technologists and Technicians, All Other
29-9092	Genetic Counselors *
29-9099	Healthcare Practitioners and Technical Workers, All Other
31-1014	Nursing Assistants
31-1015	Orderlies *

31-9097	Phlebotomists *
31-9099	Healthcare Support Workers, All Other
33-9032	Security Guards
33-9093	Transportation Security Screeners *
33-9099	Protective Service Workers, All Other
39-4031	Morticians, Undertakers, and Funeral Directors*
41-9099	Sales and Related Workers, All Other
43-3099	Financial Clerks, All Other *
43-9199	Office and Administrative Support Workers, All Other
47-2111	Electricians
47-2181	Roofers
47-2231	Solar Photovoltaic Installers*
47-4099	Construction and Related Workers, All Other
49-9021	Heating, Air Conditioning, and Refrigeration Mechanics and Installers
49-9081	Wind Turbine Service Technicians*
49-9099	Installation, Maintenance, and Repair Workers, All Other
51-3099	Food Processing Workers, All Other *
51-5112	Printing Press Operators
51-5113	Print Binding and Finishing Workers
51-9151	Photographic Process Workers and Processing Machine Operators
51-9199	Production Workers, All Other

SOC codes no longer in use

Of the 821 detailed SOC codes in the 2000 SOC, the 40 listed in table 2 are not used in the 2010 SOC. For each detailed 2000 SOC occupation, the corresponding 2010 codes and titles are also shown.

Table 2: 2000 SOC codes no longer in use and their 2010 replacements

2000 SOC code	2000 SOC title	2010 SOC code	2010 SOC title
11-3041	Compensation and Benefits Managers	11-3111	Compensation and Benefits Managers
11-3042	Training and Development Managers	11-3131	Training and Development Managers
11-3049	Human Resources Managers, All Other	11-3121	Human Resources Managers
11-9011	Farm, Ranch, and Other Agricultural Managers	11-9013	Farmers, Ranchers, and Other Agricultural Managers
11-9012	Farmers and Ranchers	11-9013	Farmers, Ranchers, and Other Agricultural Managers
13-1061	Emergency Management Specialists	11-9161	Emergency Management Directors
13-1072	Compensation, Benefits, and Job Analysis Specialists	13-1141	Compensation, Benefits, and Job Analysis Specialists
13-1073	Training and Development Specialists	13-1151	Training and Development Specialists
13-1079	Human Resources, Training, and Labor Relations Specialists, All Other	13-1075	Labor Relations Specialists
15-1011	Computer and Information Scientists, Research	15-1111	Computer and Information Research Scientists
15-1021	Computer Programmers	15-1131	Computer Programmers
15-1031	Computer Software Engineers, Applications	15-1132	Software Developers, Applications

Table 2 (con't): 2000 SOC codes no longer in use and their 2010 replacements

15-1032	Computer Software Engineers, Systems Software	15-1133	Software Developers, Systems Software
15-1041	Computer Support Specialists	15-1151	Computer User Support Specialists
15-1051	Computer Systems Analysts	15-1143	Computer Network Architects (part)
		15-1121	Computer Systems Analysts
15-1061	Database Administrators	15-1141	Database Administrators
15-1071	Network and Computer Systems Administrators	15-1142	Network and Computer Systems Administrators (part)
15-1081	Network Systems and Data Communications Analysts	15-1122	Information Security Analysts
		15-1134	Web Developers
		15-1142	Network and Computer Systems Administrators (part)
		15-1143	Computer Network Architects (part)
		15-1152	Computer Network Support Specialists
15-1099	Computer Specialists, All Other	15-1199	Computer Occupations, All Other
19-3021	Market Research Analysts	13-1161	Market Research Analysts and Marketing Specialists
23-2092	Law Clerks	23-1012	Judicial Law Clerks
		23-2011	Paralegals and Legal Assistants (part)
25-2041	Special Education Teachers, Preschool, Kindergarten, and Elementary School	25-2051	Special Education Teachers, Preschool
		25-2052	Special Education Teachers, Kindergarten and Elementary School
25-2042	Special Education Teachers, Middle School	25-2053	Special Education Teachers, Middle School
25-2043	Special Education Teachers, Secondary School	25-2054	Special Education Teachers, Secondary School
29-1111	Registered Nurses	29-1141	Registered Nurses
29-1121	Audiologists	29-1181	Audiologists
31-1012	Nursing Aides, Orderlies, and Attendants	31-1014	Nursing Assistants
		31-1015	Orderlies
39-6021	Tour Guides and Escorts	39-7011	Tour Guides and Escorts
39-6022	Travel Guides	39-7012	Travel Guides
39-6031	Flight Attendants	53-2031	Flight Attendants
39-6032	Transportation Attendants, Except Flight Attendants and Baggage Porters	53-6061	Transportation Attendants, Except Flight Attendants
45-1012	Farm Labor Contractors	13-1074	Farm Labor Contractors
49-9042	Maintenance and Repair Workers, General	49-9071	Maintenance and Repair Workers, General
51-5011	Bindery Workers	51-5113	Print Binding and Finishing Workers (part)
51-5012	Bookbinders	51-5113	Print Binding and Finishing Workers (part)
51-5021	Job Printers	51-5112	Printing Press Operators (part)
		51-5113	Print Binding and Finishing Workers (part)
51-5022	Prepress Technicians and Workers	51-5111	Prepress Technicians and Workers
51-5023	Printing Machine Operators	51-5112	Printing Press Operators (part)
51-9131	Photographic Process Workers	51-9151	Photographic Process Workers and Processing Machine Operators
51-9132	Photographic Processing Machine Operators	51-9151	Photographic Process Workers and Processing Machine Operators

Classification Principles

The SOC Classification Principles form the basis on which the SOC system is structured.

1. The SOC covers all occupations in which work is performed for pay or profit, including work performed in family-operated enterprises by family members who are not directly compensated. It excludes occupations unique to volunteers. Each occupation is assigned to only one occupational category at the lowest level of the classification.

2. Occupations are classified based on work performed and, in some cases, on the skills, education, and/or training needed to perform the work at a competent level.

3. Workers primarily engaged in planning and directing are classified in management occupations in Major Group 11-0000. Duties of these workers may include supervision.

4. Supervisors of workers in Major Groups 13-0000 through 29-0000 usually have work experience and perform activities similar to those of the workers they supervise, and therefore are classified with the workers they supervise.

5. Workers in Major Group 31-0000 Healthcare Support Occupations assist and are usually supervised by workers in Major Group 29-0000 Healthcare Practitioners and Technical Occupations. Therefore, there are no first-line supervisor occupations in Major Group 31-0000.

6. Workers in Major Groups 33-0000 through 53-0000 whose primary duty is supervising are classified in the appropriate first-line supervisor category because their work activities are distinct from those of the workers they supervise.

7. Apprentices and trainees are classified with the occupations for which they are being trained, while helpers and aides are classified separately because they are not in training for the occupation they are helping.

8. If an occupation is not included as a distinct detailed occupation in the structure, it is classified in an appropriate "All Other," or residual, occupation. "All Other" occupations are placed in the structure when it is determined that the detailed occupations comprising a broad occupation group do not account for all of the workers in the group. These occupations appear as the last occupation in the group with a code ending in "9" and are identified in their title by having "All Other" appear at the end.

9. The U.S. Bureau of Labor Statistics and the U.S. Census Bureau are charged with collecting and reporting data on total U.S. employment across the full spectrum of SOC major groups. Thus, for a detailed occupation to be included in the SOC, either the Bureau of Labor Statistics or the Census Bureau must be able to collect and report data on that occupation.

Coding Guidelines

The SOC Coding Guidelines are intended to assist users in consistently assigning SOC codes and titles to survey responses and in other coding activities.

1. A worker should be assigned to an SOC occupation code based on work performed.

2. When workers in a single job could be coded in more than one occupation, they should be coded in the occupation that requires the highest level of skill. If there is no measurable difference in skill requirements, workers should be coded in the occupation in which they spend the most time. Workers whose job is to teach at different levels (e.g., elementary, middle, or secondary) should be coded in the occupation corresponding to the highest educational level they teach.

3. Data collection and reporting agencies should assign workers to the most detailed occupation possible. Different agencies may use different levels of aggregation, depending on their ability to collect data. For more information on data produced using the SOC, see the Frequently Asked Questions (FAQs) section.

4. Workers who perform activities not described in any distinct detailed occupation in the SOC structure should be coded in an appropriate "All Other" or residual occupation. These residual occupational categories appear as the last occupation in a group with a code ending in "9" and are identified by having the words "All Other" appear at the end of the title.

5. Workers in Major Groups 33-0000 through 53-0000 who <u>spend 80 percent or more of their time performing supervisory activities</u> are coded in the appropriate first-line supervisor category in the SOC. In these same Major Groups (33-0000 through 53-0000), persons with supervisory duties who <u>spend less than 80 percent of their time supervising</u> are coded with the workers they supervise.

6. Licensed and non-licensed workers performing the same work should be coded together in the same detailed occupation, except where specified otherwise in the SOC definition.

Standard Occupational Classification and Coding Structure

The occupations in the SOC are classified at four levels of aggregation to suit the needs of various data users: major group, minor group, broad occupation, and detailed occupation. Each lower level of detail identifies a more specific group of occupations. The 23 major groups, listed below, are divided into 97 minor groups, 461 broad occupations, and 840 detailed occupations.

2010 SOC Major Groups

Code	Title
11-0000	Management Occupations
13-0000	Business and Financial Operations Occupations
15-0000	Computer and Mathematical Occupations
17-0000	Architecture and Engineering Occupations
19-0000	Life, Physical, and Social Science Occupations
21-0000	Community and Social Service Occupations
23-0000	Legal Occupations
25-0000	Education, Training, and Library Occupations
27-0000	Arts, Design, Entertainment, Sports, and Media Occupations
29-0000	Healthcare Practitioners and Technical Occupations
31-0000	Healthcare Support Occupations
33-0000	Protective Service Occupations
35-0000	Food Preparation and Serving Related Occupations
37-0000	Building and Grounds Cleaning and Maintenance Occupations
39-0000	Personal Care and Service Occupations
41-0000	Sales and Related Occupations
43-0000	Office and Administrative Support Occupations
45-0000	Farming, Fishing, and Forestry Occupations
47-0000	Construction and Extraction Occupations
49-0000	Installation, Maintenance, and Repair Occupations
51-0000	Production Occupations
53-0000	Transportation and Material Moving Occupations
55-0000	Military Specific Occupations

Some users may require aggregations other than the SOC system built on these major groups. Further details on alternate occupational aggregations and approved modifications to the SOC structure are provided in the following section on page xviii.

Major groups are broken into minor groups, which, in turn, are divided into broad occupations. Broad occupations are then divided into one or more detailed occupations.

> 29-0000 Healthcare Practitioners and Technical Occupations
> 29-1000 Health Diagnosing and Treating Practitioners
> 29-1060 Physicians and Surgeons
> 29-1062 Family and General Practitioners

- o Major group codes end with 0000 (e.g., 29-0000 Healthcare Practitioners and Technical Occupations).

- o Minor groups generally end with 000 (e.g., 29-1000 Health Diagnosing and Treating Practitioners)—the exceptions are minor groups 15-1100 Computer Occupations and 51-5100 Printing Workers, which end with 00.
- o Broad occupations end with 0 (e.g., 29-1060 Physicians and Surgeons).
- o Detailed occupations end with a number other than 0 (e.g., 29-1062 Family and General Practitioners).

Each item in the SOC is designated by a six-digit code. The hyphen between the second and third digit is used only for clarity (see figure 1).

Figure 1.

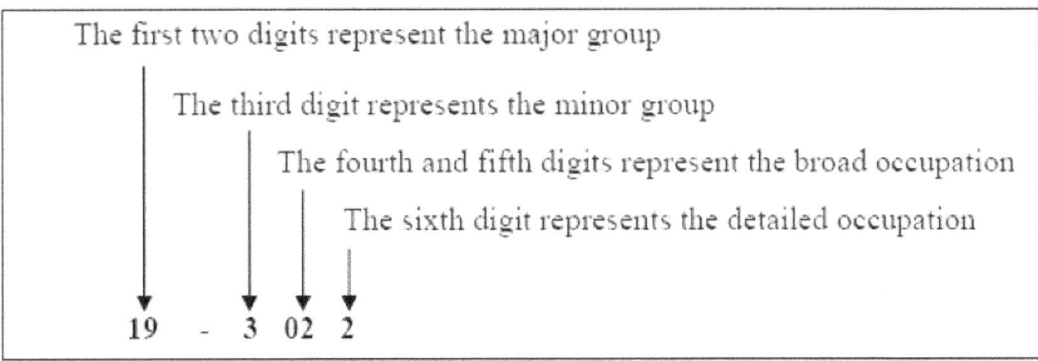

As shown in figure 2, all residuals ("Other," "Miscellaneous," or "All Other" occupations), whether at the detailed or broad occupation or minor group level, contain a "9" at the level of the residual. Minor groups that are major group residuals end in 9000 (e.g., 33-9000, Other Protective Service Workers). Broad occupations that are minor group residuals end in 90 (e.g., 33-9090, Miscellaneous Protective Service Workers). Detailed residual occupations end in 9 (e.g., 33-9099, Protective Service Workers, All Other).

Figure 2.

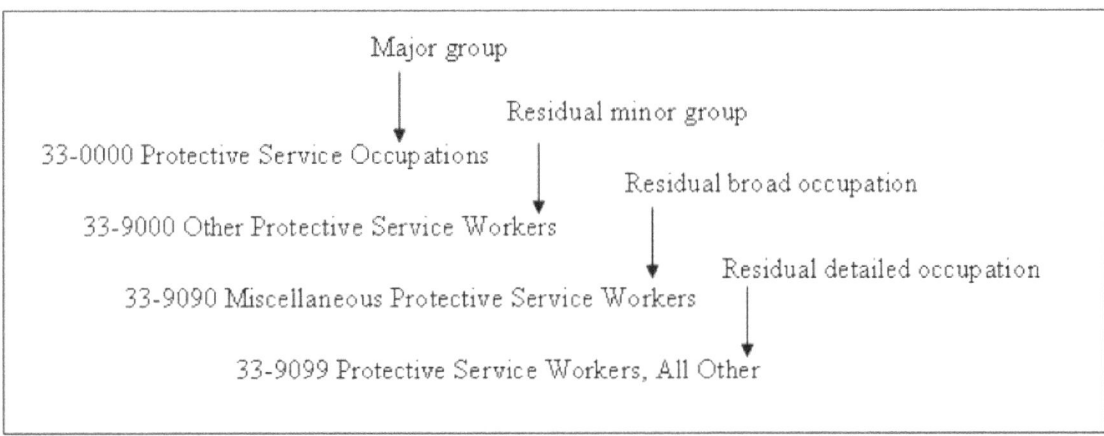

If there are more than nine broad occupations in a minor group (e.g., 51-9000 Other Production Occupations); or more than eight, if there is no residual (e.g., 47-2000 Construction Trades Workers), then the code xx-x090 is skipped (reserved for residuals), the code xx-x000 is skipped (reserved for minor groups), and the numbering system will continue with code xx-x110. The residual broad occupation is then code xx-x190 or xx-x290 (e.g., 51-9190, Miscellaneous Production Workers).

The structure is comprehensive, and encompasses all occupations in the U.S. economy. If a specific occupation is not listed, it is included in a residual category with similar occupations.

Detailed occupations are identified and defined so that each occupation includes workers who perform similar job tasks as described in Classification Principle 2. Definitions begin with the duties all workers in the occupation perform. Some definitions include a sentence at the end describing tasks workers in an occupation *may*, but do not necessarily *have to* perform, in order to be included in the occupation. Where the definitions include tasks also performed by workers in another occupation, cross-references to that occupation are provided in the definition.

Figure 3 identifies the eight elements that appear in detailed SOC occupations. All six-digit, detailed occupations have a SOC code (1), a title (2), and a definition (3). All workers classified in an occupation are required to perform the duties described in the first sentence of each definition (4). Some definitions also have a "may" statement (5), an "includes" statement (6), and/or an "excludes" statement (7). Many occupations have one or more "illustrative examples" (8), presented in alphabetical order. Illustrative examples are job titles classified in only that occupation, and were selected from the Direct Match Title File described on page iv.

Figure 3.

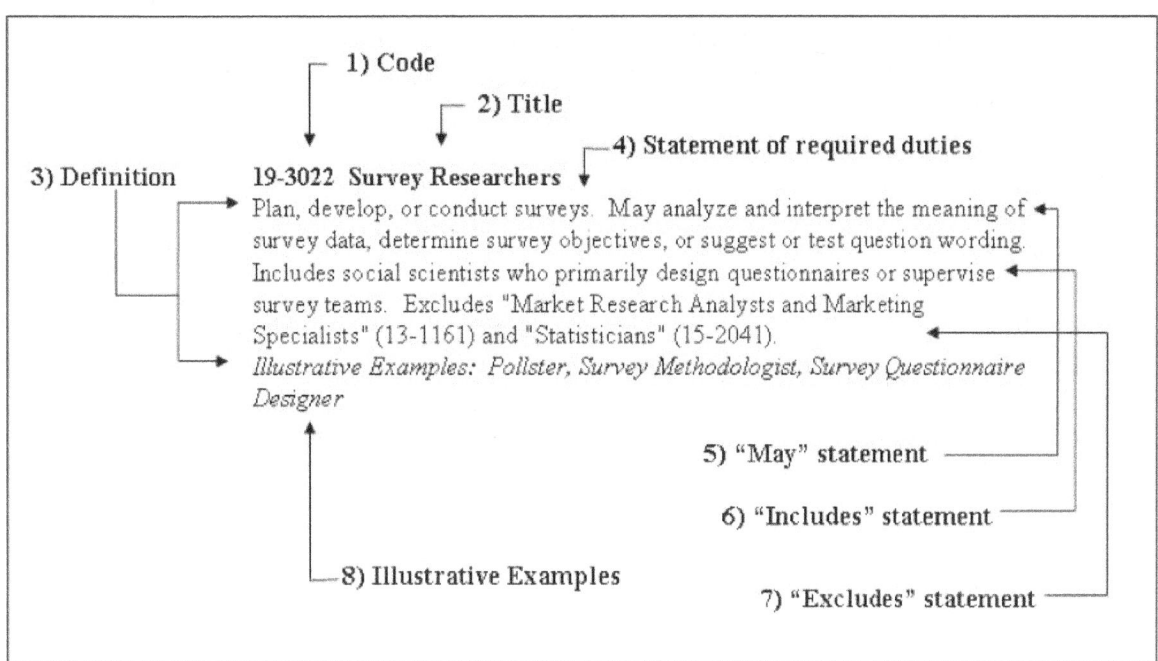

The "may" statement describes tasks that workers in that occupation may – but are not required to – perform in order to be classified with Survey Researchers. The "includes" statement identifies particular workers who should be classified with Survey Researchers. The "excludes" statement indicates other detailed occupations that may be similar to Survey Researchers and clarifies that workers who fall into those occupations should be excluded from Survey Researchers.

Approved Modifications to the Structure

Agencies may use the SOC or parts of the SOC at varying levels of the system. For example, data may be collected at the broad occupation level in some areas and at the detailed level in others.

Occupations below the detailed level

The coding system is designed to allow SOC users desiring a delineation of occupations below the detailed occupation level to use a decimal point and additional digit(s) after the sixth digit. For example, Secondary School Teachers, Except Special and Career/Technical Education (25-2031) is a detailed occupation. Agencies wishing to collect more particular information on teachers by subject matter might use 25-2031.1 for secondary school science teachers or 25-2031.12 for secondary school biology teachers. Additional levels of detail also may be used to distinguish workers who have different training or years of experience.

OMB recommends that those needing extra detail use the structure of the Department of Labor's Employment and Training Administration's Occupational Information Network (O*NET). For more information, see http://online.onetcenter.org.

Higher levels of aggregation

Some users may wish to present occupational data at higher levels of aggregation than the SOC major groups. To meet this need and to maintain consistency and comparability across data sets, either the intermediate or the high-level aggregations presented in tables 3 and 4 should be used for data tabulation purposes.

Table 3. Intermediate aggregation to 13 groups, 2010 SOC

Intermediate aggregation	Major groups included	Intermediate aggregation title
1	11-13	Management, Business, and Financial Occupations
2	15-19	Computer, Engineering, and Science Occupations
3	21-27	Education, Legal, Community Service, Arts, and Media Occupations
4	29	Healthcare Practitioners and Technical Occupations
5	31-39	Service Occupations
6	41	Sales and Related Occupations
7	43	Office and Administrative Support Occupations
8	45	Farming, Fishing, and Forestry Occupations
9	47	Construction and Extraction Occupations
10	49	Installation, Maintenance, and Repair Occupations
11	51	Production Occupations
12	53	Transportation and Material Moving Occupations
13	55	Military Specific Occupations

Table 4. High-level aggregation to 6 groups, 2010 SOC

High-level aggregation	Major groups included	High-level aggregation title
1	11-29	Management, Business, Science, and Arts Occupations
2	31-39	Service Occupations
3	41-43	Sales and Office Occupations
4	45-49	Natural Resources, Construction, and Maintenance Occupations
5	51-53	Production, Transportation, and Material Moving Occupations
6	55	Military Specific Occupations

Alternate aggregations

Data collection issues or confidentiality concerns may prevent agencies from reporting all the detail indicated in the SOC. For example, an agency might report the detail of at least one occupational category at a particular level of the SOC structure but must aggregate the other occupations at that level. In such cases, the agency may adjust the occupational categories so long as these adjustments permit aggregation to the next higher SOC level. In such a situation, agencies must distinguish such groups from the official SOC aggregation. If agencies choose this option they must obtain approval from the Standard Occupational Classification Policy Committee for their proposed aggregation scheme.

Frequently Asked Questions

1. How do the U.S. Bureau of Labor Statistics and the Census Bureau determine if they can collect and report on an occupation? (See Classification Principle 9.)

The Bureau of Labor Statistics (BLS) develops estimates of occupational employment and wages for wage and salary workers in nonfarm establishments in its Occupational Employment Statistics (OES) Survey. This survey collects information from business establishments sampled by industry and geographic area. BLS looks at the definition, and at the size and dispersion of (estimated) employment, in determining whether it can collect and report data on an occupation. For OES survey respondents to report on an occupation, the duties or work performed of the occupation must be uniquely defined, i.e., clearly differentiated from those of any other occupations. If the occupation is widely dispersed across areas and/or industries, employment in an occupation must be sizeable to be reliably measured. If the occupation is highly concentrated in a single industry or area, smaller levels of employment can be reliably measured.

The Census Bureau develops estimates of occupational employment of the population with its household-based Current Population (a joint program with BLS) and American Community Surveys. As with BLS above, the Census Bureau is concerned about the size and dispersion of employment in an occupation in determining if it can collect and report data on that occupation. In addition, the Census Bureau considers whether the respondents to its household surveys, who may provide information for themselves as well as for other household members, are likely to report the job titles and job activities associated with an occupation accurately and completely. Household survey respondents tend to give general or informal, rather than specific or technical, occupational titles. For example, a household survey respondent may report "doctor," rather than "pediatrician." This makes it difficult for the Census Bureau to report on such specialized occupations.

2. What is the difference between an occupation and a job?

An occupation is a category of jobs that are similar with respect to the work performed and the skills possessed by the incumbents. A job is the specific set of tasks performed by an individual worker. "Turnpike toll collector" is an example of a job that corresponds to the occupation 41-2011 Cashiers.

3. Why doesn't every job title have its own code in the SOC?

Occupational classification schemes examine and organize the millions of jobs and tens of thousands of job titles in the economy into occupations based upon their similarities as determined by the scheme's classification principles. The organizing principle of the SOC system is work performed rather than job title so there are many fewer occupation codes in the SOC than there are jobs in the economy.

4. What is the difference between the SOC Classification Principles and the Coding Guidelines?

The SOC Classification Principles form the basis on which the SOC system is structured. The Coding Guidelines are intended to assist SOC users in consistently assigning SOC occupational codes to survey responses.

5. Who uses the SOC?

Government agencies that collect and publish occupational statistical data use the SOC. See FAQ number 6 for more detail. At the Federal level, these agencies and programs include:

>   Department of Commerce
>>   Census Bureau
>   Department of Defense
>   Department of Education
>   Department of Health and Human Services
>   Department of Labor
>>   Bureau of Labor Statistics
>>>   Employment Projections Program
>>>   Labor Force Statistics from the Current Population Survey
>>>   National Compensation Survey
>>>   National Longitudinal Surveys
>>>   Occupational Employment Statistics
>>>   Occupational Health and Safety Statistics
>>   Employment and Training Administration
>>   Employment Standards Administration
>   Department of Transportation
>   Department of Veterans Affairs
>>   National Center for Veterans Analysis and Statistics
>   Equal Employment Opportunity Commission
>   National Science Foundation
>>   Division of Science Resources Statistics
>   Office of Personnel Management

6. Where can I get information on the occupations in the SOC?

Depending on the type of information you are seeking, you may obtain information from several agencies:

a) The U.S. Census Bureau publishes occupational data annually, collected through the American Community Survey (ACS), for the Nation, all States and the District of Columbia, Puerto Rico, and all counties and places with populations of at least 65,000. The Census Bureau also publishes 3-year ACS data for geographic areas with populations of at least 20,000 and 5-year ACS data for all geographies in the U.S. and Puerto Rico. Census 2010 will collect, classify, and publish occupational data for Guam, American Samoa, the Commonwealth of

Northern Mariana Islands, and the U.S. Virgin Islands. Other household surveys publish occupational data at varying levels of detail and geography. Standard tabulations are available through the American FactFinder via the Internet at http://www.census.gov. Information about occupation coding and written reports on occupational trends can be found at http://www.census.gov/hhes/www/ioindex/ioindex.html. For additional information, contact the Census Bureau's Question and Answer Center at http://ask.census.gov or contact the Call Center at (301) 763-INFO.

b) The Department of Defense publishes data that cross-reference military occupational codes of the Army, Navy, Air Force, Marine Corps, and Coast Guard with civilian equivalent occupations. Additional information on available data products can be obtained on the Internet at http://www.dmdc.osd.mil; or by writing to Director, Defense Manpower Data Center, 1600 Wilson Blvd., Suite 400, Arlington, VA 22209-2593.

c) The National Center for Education Statistics (NCES) publishes data collected through the School and Staffing Survey (SASS) on the employment of elementary and secondary teachers, principals, and other school staff, as well as detailed information on their education, training, and background characteristics. NCES publishes detailed data on postsecondary instructors and professors collected through the Integrated Postsecondary Education Data System (IPEDS). In addition, NCES conducts various longitudinal studies that follow high school and college students into their working years and uses the SOC to classify their occupations. Products based on data from these various surveys and programs are available from the specific surveys and programs, which can be found at http://nces.ed.gov/surveys.

d) Biennially, the Bureau of Labor Statistics' Employment Projections (EP) Program publishes the *Occupational Outlook Handbook* and *Career Guide to Industries*. In addition, EP publishes the *Occupational Outlook Quarterly*. For more information about these publications, visit the EP Web site at http://www.bls.gov/emp or contact the Chief, Division of Occupational Outlook, Bureau of Labor Statistics, 2 Massachusetts Ave. NE., Room 2135, Washington, DC 20212, telephone (202) 691-5700.

e) The Current Population Survey (CPS), a joint program of the Census Bureau and the Bureau of Labor Statistics, uses the 2002 Census occupational classification system, which is derived from the 2000 Standard Occupational Classification. CPS data series are available on this classification beginning with year 2000. The CPS previously used the 1990 Census occupational classification, which was adapted from the 1980 SOC. CPS data series on the earlier classification are available from 1983-2002; these data are not directly comparable with the current series. The Bureau of Labor Statistics publishes national-level estimates of occupational employment, unemployment, and earnings with demographic detail from the CPS. The CPS homepage on the BLS website is at http://www.bls.gov/cps/home.htm; contact information for the BLS CPS program can be found at http://www.bls.gov/cps/contact.htm.

f) The Bureau of Labor Statistics' National Compensation Survey (NCS) program provides comprehensive measures of occupational wages; employment cost trends; and benefit incidence and detailed plan provisions. Detailed occupational earnings are available for selected metropolitan and nonmetropolitan areas, nine Census divisions, and on a National basis. Employment cost trends and information on the incidence and detailed provision of employee benefit plans are published for major occupational groups. For more information, see the NCS Web site at http://www.bls.gov/ncs/home.htm, call (202) 691-6199, or send an e-mail to NCSInfo@bls.gov. Correspondence may be sent to U.S. Bureau of Labor Statistics National Compensation Survey, 2 Massachusetts Ave., NE., Room 4175, Washington, DC 20212-0001.

g) The Bureau of Labor Statistics' Occupational Employment Statistics (OES) program produces cross-industry occupational employment and wage estimates for the Nation, all States, the District of Columbia, Guam, Puerto Rico, the U.S. Virgin Islands, metropolitan areas, metropolitan divisions, and nonmetropolitan areas. OES also publishes national industry-specific occupational employment and wage estimates for sectors and 3-, 4-, and selected 5-digit North American Industry Classification System (NAICS) industries. Data are available from the OES home page at http://www.bls.gov/oes/home.htm. For assistance with these data, contact the OES program at (202) 691-6569 or oesinfo@bls.gov. Industry-specific data for States and metropolitan and nonmetropolitan areas may be available from the State workforce agencies by contacting the individual State or States for which information is needed. Contact information for the State workforce agencies is available at http://www.bls.gov/bls/ofolist.htm.

h) The Employment and Training Administration's (ETA) Occupational Information Network (O*NET) system is a comprehensive database of occupational competency profiles. ETA sponsors the development, updating, and dissemination of O*NET information through a grant with the North Carolina Employment Security Commission. The O*NET system is based on the Standard Occupational Classification (SOC) system and also provides information on additional detailed occupations within a SOC category in selected instances. The O*NET Content Model of occupational descriptors is the foundation for a series of survey questionnaires that go out to incumbent workers in various occupations which form the basis for the O*NET occupational competency profiles. The O*NET system is the successor to the Dictionary of Occupational Titles, which was last published by the Department of Labor in 1991. O*NET information is available via the Internet at http://online.onetcenter.org and also as a downloadable electronic database from the O*NET Resource Center: http://www.onetcenter.org/database.html. For more information, contact O*NET Customer Support at onet@ncmail.net or contact the Department of Labor at o-net@dol.gov . You can also write to the O*NET project director at Office of

Workforce Investment, Employment and Training Administration, U.S. Department of Labor, FPB Room S 4231, 200 Constitution Ave., NW., Washington, DC 20210.

i) The Equal Employment Opportunity Commission (EEOC) uses SOC occupational classifications, and equivalent Census occupational classifications, to create broader categories as part of the Commission's data survey and enforcement programs. Under the survey program, employer workforce information is collected periodically from private-sector firms on the Employer Information Report (EEO-1), and public sector employers on the State and Local Government Report (EEO-4). More information may be obtained from the Commission's Web site at http://www.eeoc.gov.

j) The National Science Foundation (NSF) Division of Science and Resources Statistics (SRS) Web site provides access to the Scientists and Engineers Statistical Data System (SESTAT), a comprehensive and integrated system of information about the employment, educational and demographic characteristics of scientists and engineers in the United States. It is intended for both policy analysis and general research, having features for both the casual and more intensive data user. More information may be obtained from the SESTAT Web site at http://www.nsf.gov/statistics/sestat.

7. Whom should I contact if I have a question about the SOC?

You may call the SOC information line at 202-691-6500, or send an e-mail to SOC@bls.gov.

8. Why are there different levels of detail in the SOC?

The four-tiered levels in the SOC enable users to choose the level or levels of detail corresponding to their interest and ability to collect data on different occupations. Users needing different levels of detail will still be able to compare data at the defined levels. Please see the description of alternative aggregations on pages xviii-xix for more information.

9. Why can't I find my job title in the SOC?

This volume lists occupations that may have many different job titles. It does not attempt to provide an exhaustive list of job titles. A list of additional titles called the Direct Match title file is available at http://www.bls.gov/soc. If your title is not listed, you may e-mail SOC@bls.gov to suggest its inclusion.

10. Which occupations in the SOC cover "professionals"?

The 2010 SOC does not classify or identify workers using the term "professional", or other similar terms such as "skilled" or "unskilled." The SOC was created solely for statistical purposes (see FAQ number 13) and the classification structure is not intended to rank or group occupations by education, credentials, earnings, or any other similar user-defined indicator of status. However, government agencies or private users may define and use various terms to suit their own purposes. For example, the Employment and Training Administration's O*NET program classifies occupations into 1 of 5 "job zones," based on data regarding the levels of education, experience, and training needed for work in an occupation, ranging from "little or no" to "extensive" preparation (for more information, see http://online.onetcenter.org/help/online/zones).

11. Why are supervisors of workers in Major Groups 13-0000 through 31-0000 not listed? Where should they be classified?

Supervisors of workers in Major Groups 13-0000 through 29-0000 are classified with the occupations they supervise because they often must have the same type of training, education, and experience as the workers they supervise. Supervisors of workers in Major Group 31-0000 are usually classified in Major Group 29-0000. See Classification Principles 4 and 5 on page xii.

12. When is the next revision of the SOC scheduled?

The next major review and revision of the SOC is expected to begin in 2013 in preparation for the 2018 SOC. The intent of this revision schedule is to minimize disruption to data providers, producers, and users by promoting simultaneous adoption of revised occupational and industry classification systems for those data series that use both. Given the multiple interdependent programs that rely on the SOC, this is best accomplished by timing revisions of the SOC for the years following North American Industry Classification System (NAICS) revisions, which occur for years ending in 2 and 7. The next such year is 2018, which has the additional benefit of coinciding with the beginning year of the American Community Survey 5-year set of surveys that bracket the 2020 Decennial Census. Thus, OMB intends to consider revisions of the SOC for 2018 and every 10 years thereafter.

To ensure that the successful efforts of the SOCPC continue and that the SOC reflects the structure of the changing workforce, the SOCPC will continue its service as a standing committee. The SOCPC will meet periodically to monitor the implementation of the 2010 SOC across Federal agencies. This consultation will include regularly scheduled interagency communication to ensure a smooth transition to the 2010 SOC. The SOCPC will also perform SOC maintenance functions, such as recommending clarifications of the SOC occupational definitions, placement of new occupations within the existing structure, and updating title files.

13. Can the SOC be used for nonstatistical purposes?

The 2010 SOC was designed solely for statistical purposes. Although it is likely that the 2010 SOC also will be used for various nonstatistical purposes (e.g., for administrative, regulatory, or taxation functions), the requirements of government agencies or private users that choose to use the 2010 SOC for nonstatistical purposes have played no role in its development, nor will OMB modify the classification to meet the requirements of any nonstatistical program.

Consequently, the 2010 SOC is not to be used in any administrative, regulatory, or tax program unless the head of the agency administering that program has first determined that the use of such occupational definitions is appropriate to the implementation of the program's objectives.

14. Where can I find how the 2010 SOC relates to the 2000 SOC?

The official crosswalks can be found at http://www.bls.gov/soc. Occupations are crosswalked from the 2010 SOC to the 2000 SOC and from the 2000 SOC to the 2010 SOC.

15. Where can I obtain an electronic version or additional printed versions of the SOC?

Information from the *SOC Manual 2010* can be found on the SOC homepage at http://www.bls.gov/soc. To obtain a CD-ROM version or additional print copies of the *SOC Manual 2010*, contact

U.S. Department of Commerce
Technology Administration
National Technical Information Service
5301 Shawnee Road
Alexandria, VA 22312
(703) 605-6000 or 1-800-553-NTIS (6847)
Order Number: PB2010-105544 (hard cover)
Order Number: PB2010-500061 (CD-ROM)

16. When will Federal statistical agencies begin using the 2010 SOC in survey collection?

Federal statistical agencies will begin using the 2010 SOC for occupational data they publish for reference years beginning on or after January 1, 2010. However, it is important to note that for some programs, full implementation of the 2010 SOC will occur in stages, as sufficient data are needed to produce estimates at the full level of occupational detail. Contact an agency or program directly for specific information on implementation. A schedule of implementation dates for programs within the Bureau of Labor Statistics will be available at http://www.bls.gov/soc.

Acknowledgements

SOCPC Members
John Galvin, Bureau of Labor Statistics, Chair

Andrea Bright, Office of Personnel Management
Paul Bugg, Office of Management and Budget
Jennifer Cheeseman Day, Census Bureau
Joseph Donovan, Equal Employment Opportunity Commission
Barbara Downs, Census Bureau
Phil Doyle, Bureau of Labor Statistics
Pam Frugoli, Employment and Training Administration
Nimmi Kannankutty, National Science Foundation
Mary Kirk, Census Bureau (retired)
Roslyn Korb, National Center for Education Statistics
Mary McCarthy, Bureau of Labor Statistics (retired)
Mike McElroy, Bureau of Labor Statistics (retired)
Stephen Provasnik, National Center for Education Statistics
Sabrina Ratchford, National Center for Education Statistics
Steve Reardon, Defense Manpower Data Center
Tara Ricci, Office of Personnel Management
Sarah Richards, Health Resources and Services Administration
Marc Rosenblum, Equal Employment Opportunity Commission
Dixie Sommers, Bureau of Labor Statistics
George Stamas, Bureau of Labor Statistics

SOC Coordinating Team
Theresa Cosca, Bureau of Labor Statistics
Alissa Emmel, Bureau of Labor Statistics
Anne Louise Marshall, Bureau of Labor Statistics
Wendy Price, Bureau of Labor Statistics, Administrative Support

Workgroup Members

Bureau of Labor Statistics

Shane Stephens	Jim Smith
Richard Yeast	Sam Meyer
John Morton	Mark Doucette
Dee McCarthy	Reid VanNattan
Janice Windau	Laurie Salmon
Audrey Watson	Benjamin Cover
Patrick Kilcoyne	John I. Jones
Zachary Warren	Michael Soloy
Dina Itkin	Jeffrey Holt
Carrie Jones	Amy Bierer
Kinna Brewington	Fatemeh Hajiha
Jeffrey LaPointe	Mark Maggi
Cori Martinelli	Phillip Bastian
Sadie Blanchard	Douglas Braddock
Olivia Crosby	Lauren Csorny

Conley Hall Dillon
Thomas DiVincenzo
Diana Gelhaus
Sam Greenblatt
Elka Torpey
Jonathan Kelinson
T. Alan Lacey
Chester Levine
Kevin McCarron
Gregory Niemesh
Brian Roberts
Jon Sargent
Kristina Bartsch
Patricia Tate
David Terkanian
Michael Wolf
Ian Wyatt

Tamara Dillon
Arlene Dohm
Kathleen Green
Jeffrey Gruenert
Henry Kasper
Jill Lacey
William Lawhorn
C. Brett Lockard
Roger Moncarz
Alice Ramey
Erik Savisaar
Terry Schau
Lynn Shniper
Colleen Teixeira Moffat
Nicholas Terrell
Benjamin Wright

Census Bureau
Marisa Hotchkiss

Defense Manpower Data Center
Dawn De-iongh
Sue Hay

Employment and Training Administration
Tracie Hamilton

Health Resources and Services Administration
Jim Cultice
Annette Debisette
Jerilyn Glass
Anjum Rishi
Young Song

National Center for Education Statistics
Michelle Coon

National Center for O*NET Development
Phil Lewis
David Rivkin
John Nottingham

National Science Foundation
Kelly Kang

Office of Personnel Management
Mark Doboga